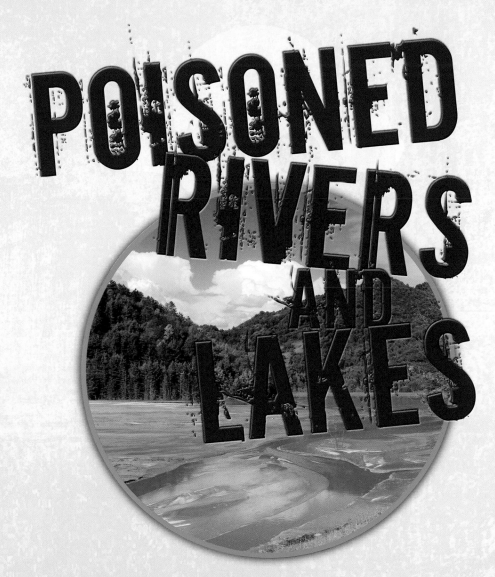

POISONED RIVERS AND LAKES

Honor Head

Gareth Stevens
PUBLISHING

Please visit our website, **www.garethstevens.com**.
For a free color catalog of all our high-quality books,
call toll free 1-800-542-2595 or fax 1-877-542-2596.

Cataloging-in-Publication Data

Names: Head, Honor.
Title: Poisoned rivers and lakes / Honor Head.
Description: New York : Gareth Stevens Publishing, 2019.
| Series: Totally toxic | Includes glossary and index.
Identifiers: ISBN 9781538235003 (pbk.) | ISBN 9781538235010 (library bound)
Subjects: LCSH: Water--Pollution--Juvenile literature.
Classification: LCC TD422.H43 2019 | DDC 363.739'4--dc23

First Edition

Published in 2019 by
Gareth Stevens Publishing
111 East 14th Street, Suite 349
New York, NY 10003

© 2019 Gareth Stevens Publishing

Produced for Gareth Stevens by Calcium
Editors: Sarah Eason and Honor Head
Designers: Paul Myerscough and Steve Mead

Photo credits: Cover: Shutterstock: Microgen; Inside: Shutterstock: africa924: p. 33;
Jose Arcos Aguilar: p. 31; alens: p. 19; alisonsgoo: p. 18b; Artush: p. 5; Deborah
Benbrook: p. 22; Ryan M. Bolton: p. 35m; Cassiohabib: p. 4 bottom ChameleonsEye:
p. 29; Clive Chivers: p. 13; condruzmf: p. 8b; K Steve Cope: p. 36t; ebenart: p. 25
bottom; ESB Professional: p. 9; hareluya: p. 36l; Leonid Ikan: p. 11t; iofoto: p. 30l;
Jet Rockkkk: p. 21t; Anna Jurkovska: p. 23b; kakteen: p. 34; Sergey Kamshylin:
p. 43; W. Kulczycki: p. 6t; Felix Lipov: p. 6b; Marktucan: p. 39t; Riccardo Mayer:
p. 16; Mikadun: p. 1; MMPOP: p. 39b; Morenovel: p. 26b; Mykola59: p. 15b; Gunter
Nezhoda: p. 32t; Inga Nielsen: p. 26t; Antonio V. Oquias: p. 42; Claudia Otte: p. 10;
Gilles Paire: p. 32b; Linda Parton: p. 41m; pcruciatti: p. 23t; Peizais: p. 40; Peresanz:
p. 7; Tomislav Pinter: p. 24bl; puwanai: p. 17t; Ricard MC: p. 37; Marco Saroldi:
p. 27t; Silent Corners: p. 15t; Mariusz Szczygiel: p. 12; JFs Pic S. Thielemann: p. 14;
Tooykrub: p. 28; Travel Stock: p. 38; wonderisland: p. 8tp; Bjoern Wylezich: p. 25t;
Kryuchka Yaroslav: p. 20.

Printed in the United States of America

CPSIA compliance information: Batch #CW19GS.
For further information contact Gareth Stevens, New York, New York, at 1-800-542-2595.

CONTENTS

 ESSENTIAL FOR LIFE

Humans and animals need fresh, clean water to live. Humans need water to drink, to grow food, to keep clean, and for sanitation, such as flushing toilets, washing, and showering. They also need water to generate electricity and for transportation. In the United States, 65 percent of drinking water comes from freshwater sources, such as rivers and streams.

We also use water in our leisure time, in sports and exercise. People visit lakes and rivers for vacations and weekend trips. Experts have found that getting close to nature, such as taking a walk by the river or sitting next to a lake, is a great way to help us relax and cope with stress and anxiety.

Visiting lakes and rivers keeps us healthy physically and mentally.

How We Get Our Water

There are many ways in which the water from freshwater sources reaches buildings. Generally, our main water supplies are pumped from rivers, lakes, or reservoirs into water towers and water treatment plants. The water towers store water, while water treatment plants use filters and chemicals to ensure that the water we use every day is safe. Water then travels through a series of underground pipes to our buildings.

Lining Up for Water

In many developing countries, people do not have access to clean water. In poorer areas and rural regions, water is pumped straight out of the ground. This water can be full of mud, germs, and chemicals, but for some people it is all they have to drink and cook with. In many countries, people wash themselves and their clothes in rivers, lakes, and streams.

In Namibia, in Africa, people have to travel miles to collect water from a public water tank. The water is pumped straight out of the ground and into the tank.

Essential for Wildlife

Animals need freshwater to drink and keep clean. Birds wash their feathers regularly to keep them healthy, so that they can fly properly. Many birds and animals breed and raise their young in forests and national parks, which have natural rivers and lakes. Rivers and lakes help to keep our air cool during long, hot summers. They also keep the ground moist, so that trees and other plants can grow.

Sparrows take a bath to clean their feathers in a fountain of freshwater.

Food Chains

Rivers and lakes are part of the food chain. They contain plants, fish, and other organisms that provide food for animals, birds, and humans. For example, crustaceans such as crayfish eat algae that grow on the riverbed. Crayfish are eaten by fish; fish are eaten by people, birds, and animals. In some parts of the world, whole communities rely on fish from local rivers or streams as their main source of protein. If food from freshwater sources is not available or is polluted by toxins, the food chain is broken. This can be harmful to both humans and wildlife.

In very hot regions in the countries of Africa, animals rely on fresh drinking water to help them keep cool.

The Water Cycle

The water cycle is the movement of water on and above our planet and underground. The sun heats the surface of large areas of water, such as oceans, lakes, and rivers. As the water warms, it evaporates into the air and becomes a vapor or gas, which rises. Trees and other plants also release moisture into the air through their leaves in a process called transpiration.

In the atmosphere, the water vapor cools, turns back into droplets, and forms clouds. As more water vapor gathers, more rain clouds form. The water in the clouds becomes bigger and heavier, and it falls back to the ground as rain, snow, hail, or sleet. The rain falls into rivers, lakes, and streams, or onto the land, forming puddles or soaking into the ground. The cycle then continues, with the sun heating the water and water evaporating into the atmosphere to become rain.

Dark storm clouds and heavy rains are part of the water cycle that keeps our rivers and lakes filled with water.

Picking Up Pollution

Runoff is water that is not absorbed into the soil and that runs over the ground into areas of water, such as lakes and rivers. Runoff often carries chemicals, toxins, oil spills, street garbage, and other pollutants it picks up from the land into the water.

Groundwater travels underground. As it travels, it picks up harmful chemicals from farm fertilizers and pesticides, human wastewater, and other sources of pollution that have seeped into the ground. Then, this is all carried into water sources, such as rivers and streams. We need clean water each day, so it is important that we keep the water in streams and rivers clean and fresh. It is also important for the health of the freshwater environment.

Polluted water pouring into a river can harm plants and poison fish and other river animals.

Waste from farm animals, such as pigs, can become part of the groundwater that runs into rivers.

Regulations

Most developed countries have strict guidelines on the purity of water used in homes, and water is tested regularly to make sure the guidelines are met. But in many developing countries where water is often scarce, there are no controls on water quality. So, in many areas, people drink, cook, and wash in whatever water is available, and much of it is seriously contaminated. The polluted water often causes epidemics and life-threatening illnesses, such as diarrhea, cholera, and dysentery.

Under Threat

There are several threats to our natural freshwater sources. Nitrogen and phosphorous are chemicals in fertilizers that are widely used on farms. These and other pollutants—such as animal manure from pigs, cattle, and sheep—get into our freshwater sources from runoff and groundwater. Homes and other buildings produce a lot of wastewater that can leak from old, damaged pipes and sewers, then find its way into freshwater sources. Rainwater falling on roofs, roads, and sidewalks washes all kinds of pollution into rivers, streams, and lakes, including plastic trash that stays in the water and slowly pollutes it over many years.

Burning Fossil Fuels

Electricity plays a vital part in almost everything we do. We use electricity for lighting, cooking, heating, to run appliances, such as refrigerators and washing machines, and to power computers and televisions. Coal, gas, and other fossil fuels are often burned to produce electricity. The smoke from burning fossil fuels can be very toxic, pumping damaging chemicals and other substances into the air. These harmful chemicals are caught up in vapor in the air and, as part of the water cycle, are rained down on the ground and directly into rivers, lakes, and oceans. Many industries that make consumer products also cause air pollution, as do exhaust fumes from automobiles.

This power plant burns coal to produce electricity. The huge chimneys pump out thick, toxic smoke, which pollutes the air.

WHO'S TO BLAME? THE TOXIC TRUTH

In July 2010, a damaged oil pipeline burst and poured crude oil into Talmadge Creek, a tributory of the Kalamazoo River in Michigan. The pipeline carries a type of oil called dilbit from Canada into the United States. Dilbit is one of the dirtiest and stickiest oils to manage. The oil sinks into the soil and pollutes the groundwater. It is costly and very difficult to remove.

Part of the Kalamazoo River was closed for a major cleanup that took around two years. The river floor had to be dredged to remove the submerged oil. Although alarms sounded in the pipeline company headquarters when the spill began, operators continued to pump oil through the pipeline. It was 18 hours before the pipeline was shut down. Nearby homes were evacuated, and wildlife was covered in oil. In 2016, Eldridge Inc., the pipeline company, paid a $177 million settlement toward restoration projects and other claims.

But who was to blame: Enbridge Inc. for not maintaining its pipes or the employees at headquarters for not responding to the alarm sooner? Was it just a case of an unfortunate accident happening? Explain how the people involved could have prevented the accident.

CHAPTER 2

WASTEWATER

• Wastewater is liquid waste that goes down a sink or a drain, from activities such as flushing a toilet, washing dishes, washing clothes, bathing, and showering. Generally, wastewater from drains is carried along pipes to a larger sewer pipe, which takes it to a sewage treatment center. Here, the wastewater goes through a series of processes that clean and treat it until it is pure enough to be sent back into a river or reservoir. Then, it becomes part of the water cycle again. Other types of wastewater include land runoff from farms, gardens, roads, and walkways, and storm water that follows heavy rain and snowfall.

This sewage treatment plant cleans and filters wastewater before it is allowed back into local lakes and rivers.

Gray, Yellow, and Black

Wastewater can be divided into three main types. Black water comes from the stuff that goes down toilets, such as toilet paper and human waste. Gray water comes from washing ourselves, washing machines, and so on. Yellow water is urine that is collected separately. Most developed countries have sanitation systems that treat and dispose of waste safely.

Untreated Waste

Many developing rural and slum communities use pit latrines. These are toilets that are a hole in the ground covered by a concrete "lid" inside a hut. Waste drops through the hole straight into the ground, where it can seep underground and end up in local freshwater sources. In some countries, untreated or partly treated sewage is pumped straight into lakes, rivers, or the ocean. This makes the water unsafe for human use, and it can harm fish and other wildlife. If wastewater damages one part of the environment or affects one link in the food chain, it can have a ripple effect throughout the whole local ecosystem and the wider environment.

In pit latrines, waste is not treated or flushed away. It can cause disease, sickness, and even death among humans.

Invisible Threats

Groundwater is one of the main sources of water supply around the world, but it is now being threatened in many different ways. Drought or long, hot summers with very little rain can dry up groundwater sources. Groundwater is pumped for use on farms to water crops and for animals to drink. Toxins from agricultural, industrial, and domestic runoff can pollute groundwater. Polluted groundwater is difficult to detect because it cannot be seen.

Groundwater can be tested to make sure it doesn't contain high levels of chemicals that might harm local waterways.

Soil and Sediment

Sediment is clay, sand, silt, and other soil particles that settle at the bottom of a river, stream, or lake, creating a thick mud-like layer. Sediment can also be made up of rotting plants and leaves, dead fish that have decomposed, and soil that has eroded near the water. Some sediment happens naturally, but with so much more construction and farming worldwide, sediment is now almost entirely made up of particles that come from human uses of land.

Sediment can affect the quality of drinking water for humans and harm wildlife in the water and on land. If the sediment becomes trapped in storm drains, it can increase flooding and the amount of polluted runoff that is washed into waterways. It makes water cloudy, so fish can't see food or predators. Murky water keeps light from getting through and stunts the growth of water plants.

Fatal for Fish

Dirty, toxic water damages environments, which can disrupt the food chain, and it harms fish and other aquatic wildlife. Sediment can clog fish gills, keeping the fish from breathing properly. This can put stress on the fish and lowers their resistance to disease, and it can slow their growth. Nutrients from fertilizers and pesticides gather in the sediment and create algal bloom that releases toxins into the water.

Contaminated groundwater has polluted this pipe.

Reducing Toxins

We can all help to reduce toxic sediment building up in waterways near us. Sweep sidewalks and driveways instead of hosing them down. Use weed-free mulch and organic fertilizers and pesticides. Wash the car on grass or gravel that absorbs water to keep the water from entering waterways as runoff.

Crude oil that has spilled into local waterways can create toxic sediment and polluted water that will kill fish and plants.

Toxic Mix

In developed countries, water is treated before it reaches households, so that it is safe to drink and use. However, traces of chemicals from everyday products, such as medicines, sunscreen, and paint, can still create a toxic mix. In developing countries, 70 percent of industrial waste is dumped untreated into waterways, making it dangerous for humans and wildlife. Drinking contaminated, polluted water puts people at risk of catching diseases such as polio, dysentry, hepatitis A, and typhoid.

Health Hazards

In 2017, the World Health Organization (WHO) stated that around the world, at least 2 billion people drink water contaminated with feces. Globally, 842,000 people—including a huge proportion of children under five years old—die each year from diarrhea as a result of unclean water. Almost 240 million people are affected by diseases passed on by parasitic worms in infected water. Children that contract sickness as a result of drinking polluted water have lengthy periods of time off school, and this reduces their chances of a better education and a more positive future.

In parts of Africa, pipes bring freshwater to rural villages. But if the water source that it comes from is polluted, the water could be dangerous.

WHO'S TO BLAME? THE TOXIC TRUTH

A lake in Bangalore, Southern India, keeps bursting into flames. In January 2018, it blazed for more than 30 hours, and a layer of ash covered nearby houses and cars. The lake is filled with toxic waste that causes it to explode into flame. About 40 percent of the city's untreated sewage flows into the lake. Residents use it as a dump for all types of garbage. Construction trucks dump huge amounts of waste in it. The lake bursts into flames, either as a result of what has been dumped into it or because of methane.

Methane is a flammable gas that builds up in water that is starved of oxygen. But who is to blame: the people who dump stuff into the lake or the local agency responsible for overseeing illegal dumping, who say their department is understaffed? Is the government to blame for not building a proper sewage system fast enough (it won't be ready until 2020)? Bangalore is a poor region struggling to keep up with the rapid growth of its cities. How would you begin to tackle water issues like this?

CHAPTER 3

DEAD ZONES

One of the biggest threats to our natural water sources are algal blooms. Scientists have been researching the causes of algal blooms for decades, and millions of dollars have been spent trying to understand why they develop. Today, more is understood about the causes, but evidence is showing that algal blooms are becoming more widespread and are increasing in size. Algal blooms are killing fish, destroying fishing areas, and polluting water that is drunk by millions of people around the world.

Algal blooms can be bright green, yellowish brown, or red. They can occur in both freshwater and ocean environments.

Algal Bloom Attack

Algae are simple plantlike organisms that are a natural part of the water ecosystem and an important part of the food chain. But when an excess of phosphorous and nitrogen gets into the water and there is a lot of sun, the alga grows out of control and produces toxins that can be fatal to wildlife and cause rashes in humans. Algal blooms cover the surface of the water and block sunlight from entering. They can also suffocate fish by clogging up their gills. When the bloom starts to die off, it takes most of the oxygen from the water, killing all life there and creating "dead zones." The rotting, dead fish can add to the algal bloom.

Toxic algal bloom can turn the water yellow and produce a nasty smell, and this can affect tourism and become very unpleasant for local residents. Toxins from the algal bloom can build up in shellfish such as scallops and clams. If contaminated shellfish are eaten, they can make a person very sick.

This otter is eating a clam, but if the clam is contaminated with toxins from algal bloom, it could harm the otter and get into the food chain.

Deadly Toxins

Nitrogen, phosphorous, and other toxins can enter the water from two sources: nonpoint source and point source. Point source pollution is when there is a definite place that can be identified as the source of the pollution. This may be a factory, a broken pipe, or a sewage treatment plant. Nonpoint source pollution is everything else, including runoff from farms, factories, sidewalks, gardens, and sediment from construction sites.

Each year, farmers spray more and more fertilizer on their crops, which builds up in nearby freshwater supplies.

Toxic Nutrients

Nitrogen is an important nutrient that helps plants grow and stay healthy. Nitrogen that occurs in nature stays at an acceptable level. However, since the mid-1980s, farmers have been using fertilizers that contain artificially manufactured nitrogen to help increase crop yields in order to feed a growing population.

This nitrogen doesn't stay in the ground but becomes part of the water cycle. This means that more nitrogen is seeping into the ground and into lakes, rivers, streams, and oceans. We use nitrogen to help crops grow to feed us, but the same nitrogen is polluting our freshwater, as well as the oceans. It is killing fish and wildlife and affecting food chains by creating algal blooms.

Water Warning!

In 2014, an outbreak of toxic algal bloom on Lake Erie in Canada caused major disruption. The local water supply was shut down. The toxic bloom caused skin rashes and burns when touched, and vomiting and liver damage if swallowed. Within a few days, it was safe to drink the water, but every year, the lake becomes covered in algal bloom again.

Toxic algal bloom is a problem that is spreading to more and more lakes throughout Canada, the United States, and around the world, especially to lakes in agricultural areas where a lot of fertilizer is used.

Fast-growing crops such as rice feed people worldwide, but they need large amounts of nitrogen fertilizer.

WHO'S TO BLAME? THE TOXIC TRUTH

Lake Baikal in Siberia, Russia, is the world's oldest and deepest freshwater lake. Once a natural beauty spot, it is now filled with toxic pollution, black slime, and foul smells; it is dying. In the past, a paper mill built on the lakeshore dumped toxic waste into it for decades. The mill closed in 2013. Tons of waste from tourist boats, including excrement and fuel, have been dumped in the lake for years. Waste from local tourist sites has not been treated properly and has drained into the lake. Dead mollusks and water plants have been found in one part of the lake.

Who is to blame: the authorities for not maintaining adequate, safe waste disposal or the owners of the tourist boats? Are the tourists who dump garbage in the water to blame or the paper mill that has dumped waste for decades? You may feel that everyone is to blame and that we each need to take responsibility for the safekeeping of our lakes.

Lakes Under Threat

Lake Naivasha in the Great Rift Valley in Kenya, East Africa, provides work, food, and water for humans, and a protected wildlife habitat for birds, plants, and fish. It is now threatened with becoming a dead zone, due to the increase in nitrogen pollution from the flower farms that surround the lake. Intense fishing, pollution from garbage, and wastewater from nearby housing, livestock, and construction works are also adding to the problems.

Water hyacinths are spreading across Lake Naivasha in Kenya, East Africa, which could seriously damage the habitat.

All this pollution is causing the growth of a species of water plant called water hyacinth, which is not a native to the lake. The toxic mix of nitrogen and other chemicals, together with the warm weather, are causing the water hyacinths to grow quickly. They are clogging waterways—used by fishermen, tourist boats, and wildlife—around the lake.

Water Crisis

China, in Asia, has spent decades building and developing cities, roads, factories, industries, offices, housing, airports, shopping malls, and so much more. It has also increased its agricultural output to help feed its growing population. All of this has resulted in a very polluted environment. China's dangerous toxic smogs have now cleared a little from some cities, but it still has a water pollution crisis. One reason why the rivers and lakes of China are so toxic is that industry has been allowed to dump chemical waste into them for decades, ignoring regulations and safety guidelines. In 2011, it was reported that one chemical company in Yunnan province dumped 5,000 tons (5,080 tonnes) of chemical waste next to a river used as a source for drinking water.

No Proper Treatment

Sewage treatment is also inadequate across China, so human waste, chemical waste, and industrial waste are becoming major sources of freshwater pollution. In some areas, local authorities have had to dig deeper wells to provide the population with drinking water because the higher-level groundwater is too polluted to use. The Chinese government is taking steps to improve the situation, installing new sewage pipelines and improved wastewater treatment plants.

In 2015, 85 percent of the water in the rivers of the city of Shanghai, China, was undrinkable.

In parts of China, fresh water is delivered to residents because their tap water has become so polluted.

CHAPTER 4

EVILS OF E-WASTE

In Inner Mongolia, in northern China, is a city named Baotou that has a large lake. Instead of being surrounded by grass and trees and filled with sparkling, clear water, the lake is surrounded by refineries that process rare earth minerals. Pipes from the factories constantly pour a thick, sludgy, radioactive, toxic waste, smelling of rotten eggs or sulfur, into the lake. The minerals are mined just outside Baotou and sent there to be processed.

Our homes are filled with electronic items. Without rare earth minerals, we would not have these goods.

Mineral Mining

Rare earth minerals are an essential part of every electronic item we use. They are in magnets inside wind turbines, earphones, and computer hard drives, and they are an essential part in smartphones and flat-screen televisions. Rare earth minerals are found worldwide, but only a few places have such large quantities that make it worth the money, time, and trouble to mine them. Baotou has huge amounts of rare earth minerals, and they have been mined here for decades.

Massive Destruction

Mining for rare earth minerals is destructive and does untold damage to the environment. First, the ground is dug up. Then, the earth is filled with a chemical mix that binds with the valuable minerals. At the processing plant, the minerals are cleaned and purified, which involves acid baths. The leftover toxic, acid wastewater is poured into the Baotou lake. The lake was once farmland that was flooded with water to create a place to dump toxic waste.

Dysprosium is a rare earth mineral. Although they are, in fact, not that rare, they are difficult and expensive to mine.

Lake of Death

The Baotou lake not only contains dangerously toxic materials but also radioactive substances that can cause cancer. There are no fish or plants in the lake, and crops can't grow there anymore. Farm animals, such as pigs, chickens, and goats, have died or become so sick they have had to be killed. The processing plants produce enormous amounts of toxic gas waste containing acid chemicals that pollute the air, land, and waterways.

Industrial plants in Batou have created a toxic wasteland in the mining and processing of rare earth minerals.

Burning Issues

Whenever we replace an electronic device, such as a television, microwave, computer, tablet, cell phone, refrigerator, or photocopier, the old one becomes garbage known as electronic waste, or e-waste. This e-waste can be difficult and expensive to get rid of because many countries have strict regulations on how to do so safely. To avoid high costs, some companies ship e-waste to the Far East, India, Africa, and China as secondhand goods. However, on arrival, they are usually found to be broken or are so old that they only work for a very short time. They then become part of a massive e-waste dumping problem. Most countries in Africa don't have e-waste recycling factories, so dump sites of damaged, rusting, burning devices pile up in open spaces, often next to lakes and rivers.

Dangerous Dumps

The local people try and salvage as much as they can from the e-waste. But the devices contain deadly materials, such as lead, mercury, and arsenic, that seep into the ground and poison the land, water, and air. People handle the waste with bare hands and offen get cuts and burns; they suffer sickness such as headaches and breathing problems. Burning the wires to get to the copper inside releases toxic fumes into the air. Many of the pieces of waste end up in rivers and lakes, polluting drinking water and killing fish and water plants.

Children as young as five scramble around dangerous dumps looking for bits of e-waste scrap (above) that might be worth something.

This man is working on a dump site in India, sifting through toxic e-waste for bits to sell.

WHO'S TO BLAME? THE TOXIC TRUTH

In 2017, up to 27 e-waste recycling sites were found to be operating illegally in the Utter Pradesh region of India. They were dumping e-waste and other toxic waste into the local Ramganga River, causing disastrous damage to the river and surrounding environment that could seriously harm the health of humans and wildlife.

India is the fifth-biggest producer of e-waste in the world but doesn't have the resources to deal with it. Who is responsible for the e-waste problem: the government for having poor e-waste laws or businesses that open illegal e-waste recycling units? Or, is it the companies that create the devices for not ensuring there is adequate knowledge and funds around the world to dispose of them safely? Could the electronics industry do more to ensure the safe disposal of the products they produce?

> Sales of electrical products are booming, but all these items will become e-waste at some time in the future.

Taking Responsibility

As the electronics industry grows and more people can afford to buy electronic devices, so e-waste becomes a massive environmental problem that affects people and wildlife in many developing countries. Some electrical companies are trying to make sure that e-waste is not dumped illegally in poorer countries but is disposed of safely. More and more companies, such as Ericsson, Apple, and Dell, accept that they have a responsibility to help keep environments safe from the dangers of e-waste.

Many electronics manufacturers have a product take-back policy that ensures electronic devices are disposed of safely and the materials recycled. But some companies only have a take-back program in states that require it by law. Others have a global take-back policy and will take other brands of electronic devices, not just their own. Some companies also have a trade-in policy. Take-back and trade-in policies should help to make sure that devices are disposed of safely without harming the environment.

Support a Steward

Try and support take-back companies when you buy a new device. Check whether the company has a take-back policy. If they don't, try somewhere else, and let them know why. There are many ways you can safely dispose of your old devices. Try not to put e-waste, such as old cell phones, in the garbage, even if it's legal where you live. The toxins in devices can last a long time and seep out into the groundwater, then into our waterways.

If your device is still working and not very old, think about donating it to a school or charity. Look for a recycler who is part of the "e-steward network." This a network that will recycle your electronic device safely and legally. They don't export to developing countries, and they can also refurbish and reuse old items.

Some electronics chain stores take back old equipment. Ask at your local mall, or look online. Cell phones are easily recycled. You can mail them to a reputable recycler or drop them into a nearby thrift store that refurbishes them for reuse.

Take your old cell phone or smartphone to a company that refubishes them for reuse for charity.

CHAPTER 5
MINING MAYHEM

These tailings ponds are at a mine in Utah. It is expensive to store toxic mining waste safely in this way, so it is often dumped.

Around the world, the earth is being plundered for its precious metals and minerals, such as gold and copper. These are found in ore that is usually deep in the ground and that can only be accessed by mining. In 2013, it was reported that mining companies dumped more than 180 million tons of toxic mine waste, or tailings, into rivers, lakes, and oceans each year.

When mining starts, any surface rock, soil, and grass is removed to reach the ore that contains the metals or minerals. The ore is mixed with toxic chemicals. The chemicals bind with any pieces of precious metal. The waste from this process creates "tailings," a toxic slurry or sludge that should be disposed of safely.

Getting Rid of Tailings

There are several ways in which mining companies dispose of tailings. Some put tailings into huge holes in the ground; others put it back into the original mine and others into lakes. Sometimes, the holes where the tailings are buried are covered with water and turned into artificial lakes. Sometimes, the wet sludge is turned into a dry, solid form and buried.

Tailings need long-term storage and monitoring because they remain a danger to the environment for decades. They can contain toxic chemicals such as cyanide and mercury, which need special safety measures to be stored safely and for a very long time. A 2013 report claimed that of all the world's major mining companies, only one had a policy against dumping waste into rivers and oceans, and none had a policy against dumping waste into lakes. In most instances, unless great care is taken now, toxic chemicals from tailings will leak into groundwater and affect soil, lakes, rivers, streams, and the ocean for generations to come.

The Rio Tinto in Spain is very acidic and has been turned a red color from all the waste from nearby mines.

Mercury and Gold

In West Africa, local people mine daily for gold. Their mining methods are devastating the landscape and contaminating the environment with toxic chemicals. One of the chemicals used to find gold is mercury, which is mixed with rock or soil in water to extract the gold. The contaminated water waste is then thrown away, usually into a river, where it settles in the water as sediment. Or it is thrown on the ground and forms into small pools. It seeps into the soil and becomes groundwater, contaminating sediment along rivers and lakes.

Sediment contains food eaten by small fish, which are eaten by larger fish, which are eaten by animals and humans. Before long, the whole food chain can be dangerously contaminated.

In Burkina Faso, West Africa, people come to dig for precious gold that will be turned into jewelry (above).

Deadly Duo

Gold miners often mix the lethal poison cyanide with mercury. The process leaves dangerous waste and toxic materials leaking into rivers. Cyanide causes vomiting, headaches, and breathing problems. It affects the brain and heart, and it can cause death.

Cyanide and mercury form a deadly duo. This mix is taken in by plants and becomes part of the food chain. In Indonesia, Asia, mercury and cyanide are used by local miners. Here, rice is the main diet, and cyanide and mercury are contaminating paddy fields where rice is grown, which could lead to a national disaster.

Cyanide Spill

In 1995, in Guyana, South America, the dam of a tailings pond leaked over 1 billion gallons (4 billion liters) of deadly cyanide slurry into the Essequibo River. It killed fish, plants, domestic animals, and wildlife, and it poisoned drinking water and farmland. The president declared part of the river an environmental disaster, and people were warned not to drink the water. Cyanide eventually evaporates, but only after it has killed wildlife and damaged habitats that could take years to become healthy again.

In Tanzania, East Africa, deadly toxic slurry pours into the river as miners work with cyanide and mercury to find gold.

Water Under Threat

Mining affects our freshwater lakes and rivers in many ways. Water is often redirected or piped from rivers and streams to mines that need thousands of gallons of water as part of the mining processes. This reduces the natural resources available to local people and wildlife, and it destroys habitats.

As a result of mining activity, local water sources, including estuaries, become polluted by water runoff from mines and contaminated groundwater. Chemicals washed into one part of a river or stream can affect the environment for miles around as the chemicals are carried along the river.

Often, roads are built before mining can begin. This results in soil being washed into local waterways, causing a buildup of sediment. Too much sediment can block rivers and lakes, smother water plants, and harm organisms in the water that are food for fish. The whole food chain can be badly affected.

Part of the freshwater environment in Guyana, South America, has been destroyed by this gold-mining operation.

WHO'S TO BLAME? THE TOXIC TRUTH

Illegal gold mining in Peru is threatening the health of humans and damaging the environment. The illegal mining has not only destroyed rain forest, it has also flooded the environment with mercury contamination. Mining is unregulated. Riverbeds are dredged, and the rock is mixed with mercury to find the gold. Local gold processing sites pump out masses of toxic air.

In 2016, the government in Peru declared an environmental emergency in Madre de Dios, southeast Peru, where illegal mining had been going on for decades. Mercury pollution was poisoning the people and the fish. Mercury poisoning affects people's nerves, digestive systems, lungs, and kidneys, and can cause brain damage in unborn babies. People have been told not to eat the local fish, which is seriously contaminated with mercury. But who is to blame: the government for allowing unregulated mining? Or the miners for using dangerous processes, even though it puts their own health at risk? How can it be stopped or made safer?

Illegal mining in Peru, South America, is polluting rivers and lakes and destroying habitats.

Toxic acid mine drainage seeps into groundwater and into lakes and rivers, killing fish and plants.

Acid Attack

Acid that pollutes waterways, soil, and the air is a major environmental issue around the world. Ore that contains valuable metals, such as copper, also contains many highly dangerous chemicals that are difficult to control. When the ore is exposed to air and water, a chemical reaction takes place that produces sulfuric acid. This is called acid mine drainage, and it can last for thousands of years, long after the mine has closed down.

Sulfuric acid reduces the quality of the water. It damages aquatic habitats, makes people sick, and becomes part of the water cycle, adding to the levels of acid rain that destroys trees and damages the environment. The acidification of lakes and rivers was first reported in the 1970s in Scandinavia. Now, thousands of lakes and rivers around the world are acidified.

Out of Balance

Acidification can result in the growth of unwanted sphagnum moss, which can form into a tight layer like a mat along the bottom of a lake. This smothers and kills aquatic plants and tiny organisms that are at the bottom of the food chain. Animals that eat food at the bottom of the food chain—such as insects—begin to disappear. When this happens, other insects can grow bigger, upsetting the delicate balance of this environment.

Fatal Consequences

Some fish, such as salmon and trout, are harmed by acidification. It can affect all stages of the fish's life cycle, such as breeding, egg laying, and the young fish. Either female fish cannot produce eggs at all, or the eggs and larvae don't grow as they should. In extreme cases, high acidification can strip the fish of its slimy coating, causing damage to the skin. Sulfide ore mining releases deadly chemicals called sulfates into the environment. Sulfates poison the habitat and are stored in the flesh of fish. If contaminated fish are eaten by expectant human mothers, it can harm the newborn babies, causing brain and kidney damage and behaviorial disorders.

In Indonesia, these sulfur miners are releasing toxic sulfur fumes into the air. Poisonous runoff harms streams, rivers, and lakes.

CHAPTER 6

RIVERS OF DEATH

Many of the world's biggest and most beautiful rivers are being poisoned to death. The Ganges River in Asia runs from the snowy mountains in the Himalayas through India and Bangladesh to the Bay of Bengal, where it enters the sea. Hindus believe that the river is sacred. They go to its shores to wash and cleanse their bodies and souls, and they also cremate their dead there. They believe that the water is very pure. But it is polluted along its entire length. Untreated human waste, household waste, raw sewage, tons of trash, and waste from factories—including toxic dyes, salts, and acids—are dumped in the river every day.

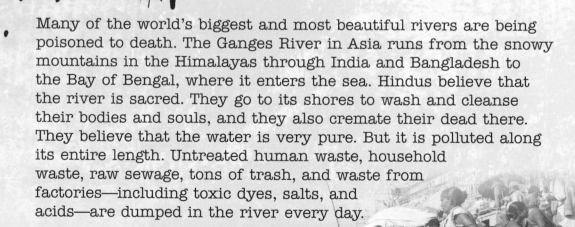

Along the Ganges River, more than 300,000 children under five die each year from diarrhea, which is caused by dirty water.

Deadly Food

There are many factories along the shores of the Ganges, and sediment near the river contains high levels of poisonous metals, such as mercury, arsenic, and chromium. In some areas, e-waste is being processed here, even though this is banned because the toxins in the e-waste are so dangerous. Farmers grow vegetables for sale in contaminated river sediment and often complain of rashes, boils, and numbness.

The Mighty Amazon

The Amazon River in Brazil, South America, snakes its way through acres of lush rain forest. But the forest is being destroyed by deforestation, dam building, and global warming, and it is poisoned by mining, logging, and farming. The Amazon supplies 20 percent of the freshwater on our planet, and it provides essential nutrients that are important to keep the rain forest land healthy.

Rare river dolphins eat mainly catfish that feed on the river floor where the deadly toxins gather. Giant otters are also under threat from loss of habitat, river pollution from mining, illegal hunting for fur, and being caught in fishing nets. Other rain forest animals—such as jaguars and tapirs, snakes, birds, and insects—rely on the river for food, water, and shelter.

The World Wildlife Fund (WWF) is using drones to monitor the numbers of rare dolphins in the Amazon River in South America.

The Nile River

The Nile is the world's longest river. It is over 4,258 miles (6,852 km) long and travels from the lakes of Central Africa to the Mediterranean Sea. Eleven countries depend on the Nile for water for use in homes, in industry, and for farming. But this precious resource is being polluted daily by a mix of toxic chemicals and deadly waste. Along its length, the Nile is polluted from several different sources, including agricultural runoff, domestic and industrial wastewater, radioactive waste, oil pollution, and contaminated groundwater. This affects both humans and wildlife, and it damages entire ecosystems.

In Egypt, people use the Nile to dump waste, wash themselves, and clean their animals, while factories dump deadly chemicals into it. A report states that in Egypt, about 38 million people drink polluted water. The same report states that people are dying of cancer and kidney failure as a result of water pollution and suffering from diseases such as cholera, typhoid, and hepatitis.

In Egypt, local people clean a motor pump in the Nile River. The pump will be used to bring fresh water to the village.

WHO'S TO BLAME? THE TOXIC TRUTH

The Flint River in Flint, Michigan, has been dangerously polluted for decades because factories have dumped all their toxic waste into the river. In 2014, the local authority in Flint decided to use the river as its source of drinking and washing water for city residents. People became sick, and their skin became blotched and burned when they came into contact with the water. One resident reported that her child's hair fell out in clumps when she took showers. At one point, the city warned residents that the water contained dangerous bacteria and should be boiled.

The city ordered large amounts of chlorine to be added to the water to kill the bacteria. This made the water more acidic, so that pipes rusted and caused dangerous levels of toxic metals, such as lead, to seep into the water. The water from faucets turned orange.

Who's to blame: those who made the decision to use a polluted river as the main source of water or local officials who ignored the tests that revealed how toxic the water was? Was it those responsible for water safety treatment? A lack of staff, money, and training are some of the reasons given. Do you think these might be valid, or are they just excuses?

In Flint, Michigan, bottled water was delivered to replace toxic tap water. However, in 2018, the governor announced this service was ending.

A Better Way

We all need to work toward keeping our water healthy. Governments can do their part by making sure that there are strong laws in place to keep industry, mining, and farming from polluting rivers and lakes. There are already many laws, but in the United States, over half of the freshwater sources—such as lakes, rivers, and streams—are considered unhealthy. Laws need to be clear, and they need to be enforced by authorities.

Many rivers run through more than one country. Some run through many countries. Polluted water from a river in one country can enter the ocean and pollute another country. Water connects us all.

International environmental organizations, such as the WWF and Greenpeace, help to raise awareness of issues that threaten the health of the people who rely on freshwater, especially in developing countries. They also monitor situations that are a danger to wildlife and the environment. Organizations like the United Nations (UN) try to bring countries together to help everyone protect the world's freshwater supplies.

In the Philippines, Southeast Asia, a river of plastic garbage has completely blocked the waterway. Nothing can survive in this.

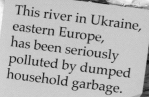

This river in Ukraine, eastern Europe, has been seriously polluted by dumped household garbage.

Facing the Future

Farmers of both large and small farms can help keep our water healthy by using less toxic fertilizers and pesticides or by changing to organic farming. Industry and factories must take control of their waste and make sure it is treated safely and disposed of properly, or they must find alternative ways to work to ensure a safer future for our water.

A major threat to all freshwater sources is untreated sewage. In developing countries, efforts to make sure that everyone has proper sanitation and that human waste is treated properly must be a top priority. Even in developed countries, sewage can end up in lakes and rivers, poisoning wildlife. Local authorities need to ensure that strict safety laws are kept, and that sewage pipes and drains are regularly checked and maintained.

Illegal mining is difficult to stop and will continue to devastate environments and pour toxins into the air and water. As consumers, we can help by cutting back on the number of electronic devices we buy. The next time you consider buying a new electronic device, make sure it is something you really need. Can you wait another year before you upgrade?

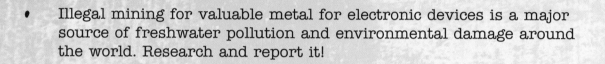

BE AN ECO REPORTER!

- Illegal mining for valuable metal for electronic devices is a major source of freshwater pollution and environmental damage around the world. Research and report it!

1 Research the Toxic Facts

- Choose an electronic device that you use every day at home or school, such as a smartphone, game console, computer, or camera.

- Research what valuable metals, such as copper, tin, or gold, are needed to make the device.

- Once you know what metals are used, track them back to their source. Have they come from mines in Borneo or Africa? Find out what is involved in extracting the metal. Draw a diagram with labels and captions to show the procedure.

- Contact the company that made the device, or do some online research. Can you find out where the company gets its metals to make the type of device you have?

- Research which toxic chemicals have been released into the environment in the process of making your item and transporting it to a store.

- Do a quick survey in your class to find out how often everyone upgrades their devices. Draw a graph to show your results. What do the results show? Do you think people upgrade too often?

- In a questionnaire, ask people if they are aware of how much damage making electronic devices costs the environment. Would they consider buying fewer devices now that they know?

② Report the Toxic Truth

Now, write a report about your findings. Send it to the manufacturer of the device. Ask them about their environmental policy when mining for valuable metals.

- Explain how mining for the metal has polluted the local freshwater supplies and harmed wildlife and the environment.

- Make suggestions for a more responsible way they could mine. Itemize some new laws and regulations.

SPREAD THE WORD

Remember, we all have a responsibility to protect our freshwater supplies. Tell your family and friends what you have learned about poisoned lakes and rivers, and share what they can do to help protect our precious water.

GLOSSARY

cholera A disease spread by consuming infected food or water.

contaminated When something is poisoned or polluted.

crustaceans Animals, usually found in water, that have a body covered with a shell or hard covering, such as crabs, shrimp, or lobsters.

deforestation Clearing a wide area of forest or woods by cutting down trees.

drones A remote-controlled aircraft that doesn't have a pilot.

ecosystem A community consisting of living and nonliving things, such as a lake that has plants, fish, water, and soil.

epidemics When illnesses or infections affect lots of people in the same area at the same time.

expectant Pregnant; expecting a baby.

estuaries Areas of water that streams or rivers flow into that joins the sea.

groundwater Water that seeps into the ground and travels underground to areas of water such as lakes, rivers, and the ocean.

hepatitis Liver damage caused by toxins.

logging When trees are cut down and stripped of their branches to prepare them for processing.

mulch Rotting and decaying organic matter, such as leaves and tree bark, which is spread on soil to improve its quality.

nutrients Substances in food that give nourishment and help keep living things healthy.

organic In farming, growing crops or feeding animals in a way that is free from artificial chemicals and as natural as possible.

refineries Places where crude oil goes to be processed and turned into oil that can be used in various ways.

runoff Water that runs over the land, ends up in drains, and eventually, reaches freshwater sources such as rivers, lakes, and the ocean. Runoff can be rain dripping off rooftops, snowmelt, water from homes and yards, and water that leaks or overflows from pipes.

sanitation The process of treating sewage and providing clean drinking water for people.

sediment Organic matter, such as leaves and twigs, that decays at the bottom of water areas, such as streams, lakes, and rivers.

slurry A runny, muddy mix of fine specks of cement, clay, or coal with a liquid, such as water or oil.

toxins Substances that can cause sickness and death in living things.

typhoid A deadly disease caused by infected food or water.

water treatment Cleaning and filtering water to make it safe.

FOR MORE INFORMATION

Books

Kaye, Cathryn Berger. *Make a Splash!: A Kid's Guide to Protecting Our Oceans, Lakes, Rivers, & Wetlands*. Minneapolis, MN: Free Spirit Publishing 2013.

Lyer, Rani. *Investigating Rivers in Crisis (Endangered Rivers)*. Mankato, MN: Capstone Press, 2015.

Stewart, Melissa. *National Geographic Kids: Water*. Washington, D.C.: National Geographic Children's Books, 2014.

Waldron, Melanie. *Rivers (Habitat Survival)*. Mankato, MN: Raintree, 2012.

Websites

kids.nceas.ucsb.edu/biomes/freshwater.htm
Learn more about freshwater habitats and the animals and plants that they support.

kids.niehs.nih.gov/topics/pollution
Check out information on freshwater pollution, plus games and activities.

www.ducksters.com/science/environment
Research more about the environment, nutrient cycles, the water cycle, habitat pollution, and global warming.

www.worldwildlife.org/habitats/freshwaters
Read about why fresh water is important and what the WWF is doing to protect freshwater sources around the world.

Publisher's note to educators and parents: Our editors have carefully reviewed these websites to ensure that they are suitable for students. Many websites change frequently, however, and we cannot guarantee that a site's future contents will continue to meet our high standards of quality and educational value. Be advised that students should be closely supervised whenever they access the Internet.

INDEX